MOTHER WAITS
FOR FATHER LATE

In memory of David Lewis Roberts
(1924 – 1992)

MOTHER WAITS FOR FATHER LATE

ANDREW BURKE

FREMANTLE ARTS CENTRE PRESS

First published 1992 by
FREMANTLE ARTS CENTRE PRESS
193 South Terrace (PO Box 320), South Fremantle
Western Australia, 6162.

Consultant Editor Thomas Shapcott.
Designed by John Douglass.
Production Manager Helen Idle.

Typeset in 10½/12pt Goudy Oldstyle by Typestyle
and printed on 90gsm Offset by
Lamb Print, East Perth, Western Australia.

National Library of Australia
Cataloguing-in-publication data

Burke, Andrew, 1944 - .
Mother waits for father late.

ISBN 1 86368 014 4.

I. Title.

A821.3

Distributed in the USA and Canada by
International Specialized Book Services, Inc., 5602 N.E.
Hassalo Street, Portland, Oregon 97213-3640, USA.

I am obliged to perform in complete darkness
operations of great delicacy
on my self.
— Mr Bones, you terrifies me.
No wonder they don't pay you. Will you die?
— My
                    friend, I succeeded. Later.

John Berryman, 'Dream Song 67'

ACKNOWLEDGEMENTS

Poems in this collection have previously appeared in the following publications: *Helix, Fremantle Arts Review, Mattoid, Overland, Phoenix Review, Quadrant, Poetry Australia, The Bulletin*, the *West Australian, Margins* (edited by William Grono, Fremantle Arts Centre Press), *Portrait* (edited by B.R. Coffey and Wendy Jenkins, Fremantle Arts Centre Press), *Wordhord* (edited by Dennis Haskell and Hilary Fraser, Fremantle Arts Centre Press).

Thanks to Thomas Shapcott for his masterly ear and eye, and to David Brooks, David Roberts and Rob Rose for earlier discussions.

The author gratefully acknowledges Writer-in-Residencies at Western Australian College of Advanced Education (1989) and Edith Cowan University (1991).

The poem 'Twenty-first Anniversary' won the Poetry Prize for the inaugural John E.V. Birch Award in 1991, conducted by the *Fremantle Arts Review*, published by the Fremantle Arts Centre.

The creative writing programme of Fremantle Arts Centre Press is assisted by the Australia Council, the Australian Government's arts funding and advisory body.

Fremantle Arts Centre Press receives financial assistance from the Western Australian Department for the Arts.

CONTENTS

SONGS & WHISPERS

WHISKERS

I shave them daily
but still they return
like weeds
along the fence of my face

Beneath my nose
(an air-conditioning unit
on the front of this building)
I cultivate a small crop
and they flow over
from the outpourings of their roots
like thin grey ferns

A semiotic critic might say
I use whiskers
as a symbol for words
everyday shaving the new crop
keeping the obvious
what's-right-under-my-nose
as my tidy poem
like a child's security blanket

and I would reply:
security and poetry are
n't seeing each other
any more
they split up
some time before
postmodernism

Another critic may say
'the poet is
metonymic, meaning
"whistlers" for "whiskers",
a jealous lover
warding the everyday lecherous eyes
off his love (who is
of course his lust-object
if only he'd admit it)'

I rejoice in
walking home from the train
scratching my chin
feeling a poem
start
among the roots

TRAILS

Rain runs over rocks
through the green hair
of mountain creeks

downriver to ocean
— rises
a mist to the sky

falls again
washing away trails
of grubs seeking
food   shelter   mate

*

Spermatozoa to ovary
we begin   we swim
in the warm waters of mother's womb

roll and tumble until
with a sticky sheen
we break free

resisting our first cry
on mother's bed of
flesh and bone

*

We criss and
crisscross
run and settle
move again

each frayed end
ends in the earth
sea or fire

SITTING TOGETHER

Those are prayers
that rise
from our windchimes

as we sit
together
in verandah shade

smoke rises
from the hills
around us

Alice cannot keep
all her songs
inside her

so she gently hums
not to interrupt
our worrying

SITTING ALONE

In this
blistering heat
I sit alone

dog's hot breath
on my barefeet
house silent

only the distant
pool filter hums

seeds are coming
alive in the earth
eggs cracking

all my unwritten
poems are rising
to be born

JUKEBOX
for Alice

My head works like a
voice-operated
jukebox: my children
say a word or phrase
and I
sing a song.

It annoys them.
It doesn't annoy them.
Some days it
does both.
They use me
to play games.

As a schoolboy
I was a prayer-wheel:
I prayed for
everything until
I wore out
my welcome.

Alice asks: 'What
sort of music was
before rock'n'roll?'
I feel it is my
parental duty
to sing for her

all the hits of
Tin Pan Alley, but
my voice is un-
sculpted, a stone
uncut, cats jump
through windows.

A BOY'S OWN CEMETERY

In Charlie's corner of our lot
stark white bricks stick out
like broken teeth:
    'R.I.P.
    Bob the Fish
    August 1988'
His charcoal words
run in the rain.

*

We bury Rufus
beneath a plum tree.
Five days later
Charlie asks: 'Will he
be bones yet?'

A skeletal dog
runs through our heads.

We discuss a dog's
relationship
with God
and if he will know us
in Heaven.

*

I say 'Regrets
make bad pets'
yet all I see
are soundless mouths
begging

*

Tonight
worms scribble
in Charlie's corner

Snug in his bed
he looks out
hears the hoot
of a midnight owl.

BANANAS

for Tom Shapcott

i)

You can't exercise on this fruit
despite its distant relationship
with monkey bars. It is bent phallic,
a late night disappointment after
the bar and all for the girl who
peeled her catsuit off like
another skin to let you in. You
were a soft, over-ripe appointment,
follied further by limp promises,
'next time' . . . As if. You hugged
the metaphor in the taxi home,
then slept on it, monkish.

ii)

My eldest sister once had a boyfriend
whose family owned a banana plantation:
yes, we teased her. Not about the phallic
implications: we were altar boys, a
banana was a banana to us. But
they were migrants, it was the Fifties.
I still call young, ripe bananas
Buzolic bananas, in this age,
the multi-cultural Nineties.

iii)

Bananas bruise easily, like children.
And isn't it just like children not
to eat bruised fruit? *Look — Daddy
eats bruised 'nanas* . . . 'Daddy'
does various foolish things, child,
doesn't mean you must. A banana
is a banana. Should it wish to be
an orange it can wish: it will
remain banana. You will be you.
Don't bruise too easily.

iv)

I wake in the morning, excited,
show my wife the poem beginning
'You can't exercise on this fruit'.
She laughs, says she'll have it later,
sliced on toast for breakfast. I
put it away. I place a Buzolic in
both the kids' lunches, warn them
not to eat on the monkey bars. They
say I'm bananas. The day begins to bend.

NEW SPIDERS

In the bathroom's musty shadows
eggs have hatched
many little spiders   rock the web
uncertain   just whose reality
is theirs

Legs wobbly   I crouch and stare

Take care spiders   he who kills ants
will wake soon   he will not hesitate
to spray and squash you   Sure he will
talk to you   as I do   but he is
young   and does not understand
life's fragility
                    Precognizance
of Buddha's word   is a tenuous web
to cling to

AROUND MIDNIGHT

11.55pm so cold
I hug myself.
Strawbroom leans against
my window knowing
tomorrow means work.
Exotic plant
looks as plastic
as its pot: dawn
will return its
veins and lifeness.
One big black fork
hangs above a
big black spoon,
ideogrammatic now.
Moths fly up and
down the panes
continuo   so
softly   crazed
by my light   as
I   attracted by
night   stare
unblinkingly   out

LAST WORDS

Play me forward
play me back

days fade
to palest grey

until a seed
of my seed's flower

catches me in mid-air
and I wake

to hear my first cry

THE FAMILY ALBUM

SONG FOR THE NEWBORN
for Jessica

In the dark hours
you bring myths
to song

in a tongue sung
before time
where you have just been

Everytime you remember
timelessness it slips
away like a favourite song

You sing it back
to dream's border
but we stopper your mouth

Listen how your
dawn birds
sing

Now   sing back

NIGHTMARE

Time takes different corners
in the dark

I was holding my baby son
he was smiling and I
hugged him   something fell
out of his mouth   I picked it
off his bib   it was his tongue
Fear froze me   I lost my tongue
grunted in fear   snorted holding it
my head thrashing   his face
smiling   his tongueless mouth open
as a cave

His tongue had come out
bloodless and warm like a fish
from the river — I stood
tongue in one hand
songless baby in the other

I wanted to wrap the tongue in a towel
but I couldn't move   speechless I couldn't
cry out   he should have cried out
his mother would have come if he had cried out
He was smiling at me   thrashing my head
fitfully holding his tongue

I wake and sweat
I flick my tongue and hear
        frogs in
        the first autumn rain

POEMS FOR JULIA

i)

Paper lies
covering
the peninsulas

of dry words, a tongue
extended ...
Pleas of time lick by.

Paperlight stands up
moving
through eyes like music —

windy night
waves
ghostflags —

paperlight shrinks
back
to the page.

Radio crackles on,
saying 'I conclude',
transubstantiating

ii)

In the closely guarded ward
sun stops
at the receptionist's feet.
An orderly let me in —
no gimmicks or fancy gifts —
just me   after work
on impulse. I
caught you wigless
four days grey growth
topping your round
flushed face —
your hand flew
to tidy lost-hair.

Across our lifetime aloofness
we kissed   your lips
tasted sweet

My last time with you
remains

iii)

You pedal me
fast to preschool before I
wet my dinkyseat

pedal fast over
Nedland's rolling greens

'What will the nuns say
if he wets his pants?!'

convent skirt and straw hat
dance in front of me

as you pedal fast
fast as you can

with your friends
making a game of it
to keep all our respects.

Tonight the peacock's
harsh bark
brings me to ground.

Your grey hair will grow
beneath earth tomorrow
fine as grass roots,

birds will fly
in your light voice
as almond blossom falls —

white silence.

To bury you we will
sing, kneel and pray.

I will bring roses
for their discipline,
a homegrown rosary.

BROTHERS
for Ray

Jokes peppered our past,
puns and shaggy dog tales

through these we praised ourselves.
Now we speak of business law

our injuries, life in
the cardiovascular ward
and cricket.

Ten years between us
I use you to pace me.

Micro-batteries pace your heart
shortening your run-up
widening boundaries . . .

Deals are not worth words
now, so we speak of
philosophies and God

AFTER YOU'VE GONE
for Ray

Crows sang   at your funeral
a gratuitous song   pines
dripped tears
of grief   of rage
Our sister made a bad joke   I
looked away

to see two rosellas walking
fronds of a giant palm:
all so calm.
I walked home   grave sand
in hand   wet with rain.
Because

you were buried Catholic
you have Italian neighbours,
a sprinkler
at your feet   How do
such facts rest in Heaven?

WHERE I LIVE

Where I live
has a tail of night flowers
that open as I turn,
close when you are near.

I hold you to own you.
You spill into
other lives,
other nights are light with you.

Where I live
is standing still
windless weatherboard sails,
shadowless sands of my heart.

I turn again
to hear you sing in empty
country halls on tour.
We teach the children their address:

old addresses
wave behind us
old loves   jazz until dawn
attendant psychiatrists and organic gardens.

Here I live
outside the city
planting trees by moonlight
hands immersed in their milk-white roots.

THE EDGE

The shortest days of the year
die bitterly.

At night now
you hear yourself in
the wind-torn darkness,
a long howl
against better-or-for-worse.

My dream is
a season ticket to New York
to live in a language
no one knows
in coldwater flats with arctic winds
up the backstairs
until one day
the Enlightened One
will appear
bearing
the quiet of the woods.

*'Do you ever seriously
think of our future?'*

We back further
into the same essentials.

I move among newspapers folded,
lifeless dolls
and silent guns —
the empty heart.

Can you dance amongst this?
my bookish silence,
weedflowers in our garden?

I wait for you
in ashlight
as the fire dies.

WARBLE ORBLE ARDLE OODLE
for Rob Finlayson

sun day is clicking with
crickets   is an island
in a sea of nast-
urtiums
last night's
webs are shoddy like
a club bar mourning after
her moaning before
i have
experience of this
and that the night brings
down on the day with its false
laughter turning into
sobs sex-
ual groans of
treasure   on broken lounges
with bad blues singers you'd
never fuck in real
light only
through this amphet-
amine glow   sores break
out and into your pissed story
like a colour or
a lie
you tell for
art's sake on the make
for fame and depression the
double-faced modern
prize   here

and there is
no history of the pre-
sent yet all lies before
the after-breath of
yes-today
we differ yet/but
all words carry their
bags as we move them about
pages leaving
trails
obvious garden
sun day setting   birds
trill down a soundtrack
crickets click
my mating
call is
a mumble   words so
short as to tear at
meaning like knives if
you want
more heart
the hear is in it
'there' is ungeographic
is never far   a
final
grunt: 'there
are you pleased now?
god knows what you've
done to us' who is
speaking?

language? wife?
are you wed to
both   bigamist of de-
sire to forever hereafter
compose?
who have
you pleased now
and when with a song of
arms and legs and nouns
and verbs
'o taste
and see' an act
of meaning wriggle like
a sheet torn with desire

A DREAM SONG

after Berryman

Inconceivably Andrew sang of night
things that end him up   falls again
so long.
— Easy, Mr Bones, they might
hears you. — Heeds me? Deaf in pain
I am to my true self   my song

a spluttery rubber balloon
down a length of room
damps
her greedless lap. My rising sap?
So much spit. They billed me
seedless   I shoot blanks.

I distress me   every day
born again in dawn's re-
erection
after wreck of night, say,
(sing) 'the pump don't work
coz the vandals took the handle'

TWENTY-FIRST ANNIVERSARY

i)

Last night I caught a mouse
trying to get back into
its cage. Call it habit,
call it pull of family,
I call it unusual. We
are sometimes at war but
we make peace. Do we
cage each other? So
long together we are twin
stars in the same sky
no matter what
phase the moon.

ii)

You might call this a
cool poem from me but
I heard a young poet
last night sound just
like me twenty years
or so ago read a love
song to his girl
sitting at a table
with his-and-her beers

He had love and lust
nicely mixed   I bet
he writes twenty love
poems a week to that
girl and if she doesn't
put a cap on his pen
he may miss out on
a rich career and
stay a woolly poet
singing the same song
twenty different ways
a week. You might call
this a cool poem from me
but I've been thinking

iii)

Huh money who needs it?
Now don't answer that one
straight away it's early
days yet only twenty one
years married so much
laughter and tears we
could always sell-up
and go bush just like . . .
but if we were gunna
we woulda by now so
let us play it one day
at a time the first be-
ing today So long together
we count our love in years

Once we loved outside of
time the physical world
spun around us which
now spins us round

iv)

Remember we sang with
Sonny and Cher in the
Lounge Bar of the now de-
funct United Services Hotel
in St George's Terrace
when the nights ran into
days and the chilly winds
blew you warm against me?
Remember the girl with
big white breasts won the
raise when you had cho-
reographed the entire
routine at the Show-Go
Discotheque? You stood up
for your rights and that
greasy Greek fired you?
Remember us? Remember them?
But now reality has inter-
fered just enough for me
to notice so let's stack
the dice our way
and roll on

ROOM SERVICE

This quiet morning
I bring you
breakfast in bed:

corn flakes,
coffee,
an orange
nasturtium
on a long stem
in a tiny
'antique' bottle

You say
I am   obvious

MAKING LOVE AT MARY'S

Awake from snoring away
hours of Spring afternoon
we sit reading in the kitchen at Mary's
as waves of jazz piano wash over us
taut strings hit by velvet hammers at
Köln January 1975 bought bootleg
in Bali 1982   re-aired in
Rockingham September 1988
tie our hearts together
measure for contra-
puntal measure   hour
on sunny hour   until
we fall into bed

and romp

POEM

Dew falls at noon

Soul breaks free
from my last will

Will our fathers
return

our love?

*

Death swims fast
in my veins
as life sings

You open
I rise

ON FINDING A GIFT OF CARROTS AT OUR DOORSTEP

Store-bought carrots have
                plastic symmetry
                        befitting their
conformity.
        No signs of
                worm's enchanting dance
no stubborn
        push
            past buried pipes.

Homegrown carrots
            grow
                a sculpture
all their own
            twisted and gnarled
                    as the hands
which grew them.
            These
                organic mystics
grew at Earth's pace
            not man's —
                    lived
a neighbourly life
            amongst woodlice
                    and bloodworms
turned orange in
            sunlight that flowed
                    through their leaves.

You pull out
      the harvest runt —
            an orange dwarf fist —
and laugh at
      the sad total
         of its struggle.

My song
      grows this way
         to you
my lyrical daughter
      as seeds
         in your garden
grow their plantselves . . .
      You help them
         grow straight
weed out
      bad neighbours
         kill a bug or three —
they flower
      like a beach full
         of umbrellas —
you're their lifeguard
      as they grow
         just as someone grew
these lumpy carrots
      to give them away
         anonymously
in a white
      plastic
         bag.

WINDING THE CLOCK BACK
for Charlie

i)

It is gone yet you bring it all back.
That grey matter in our attics
replays old tapes: how the garden Earth
flew as I drove like a demon
Maserati Number 7 — one extra push
I pass the Lotus. We rest at the pits
for a character change. As 'Grand Prix'
magazine's ace photographer
I rest my box Brownie on a sandy rise
to lift a caterpillar off the track.
Last night's rain has pitted
your backyard raceway so you are
out there now repairing it by hand
you must bring it back
flat and smooth.

Days were longer then I measured them
with a pencil pine's shadow
as it turned about my home block.
Nostalgia is the perfect weather:
I plant a tree in my grey matter
to bring it back as I hear you say
'Gentlemen, start your engines'.

ii)

Deep in night's quiet
I lay by the radio in awe
as the Aussies battled for the Ashes.
Your uncle Ray recorded every ball and run
on intricate score sheets   ball after ball
flew over the Indian Ocean   to become
heiroglyphs in pencil powder. I closed my eyes.
Someone carried me to bed with Ray Lindwall
still bowling in my head.

Weeks later
we saw 'Highlights from Lords'
grainy jumpy film at the Saturday matinee.
In these Tv days we see instant replays
of any controversy   and question
the umpire's eyesight and integrity
before the next ball is bowled . . .

Bad news good news all news is old within hours

iii)

You bring it all back
as you bowl against our wall
you do the commentary the roaring crowd
and the umpire   The game unfolds
I see you bowling at Lords
with me shouting from the boundary
your mother sewing beside me
and Ray
borrowing a score pad from St Peter

FATHER

i)

Tonight your blood rises to high tide in me

Each second your frog in my wrist jumps

You wake my fear after all these years

I want to talk through your open mouth

I want to close it   Hear me

ii)

Sit down   let's talk
I can't remember one word
you ever said to me
I can't forget your morning needles
the horror of you
puncturing your pinched stomach skinfold
as I lay in my bath before school
shrivelled in fear
breath out of rhythm
eyes stinging wide open
I washed and washed
until my navel ached

Every needle I've known since
shoots back the pain

MOTHER WAITS FOR FATHER LATE

Mother sitting at the long kitchen table
bottle and glass and book open but hardly read
waiting for Father who is as always late . . .

As always late he rolls in — I must have been
asleep upstairs and innocent at nine years — to tell
the bad news he had delayed telling: old lady dead
on Stirling Highway by his car's thump —
'She just walked out into the car, she was old,
just stepped off the curb — My bad luck
she chose me'. He drove to the pub
after police interviews,
to delay the telling of it
but told the boys in the bar well enough.

I was dreaming so who told me? I must have known
early next day before I picked up the phone
to hear a crazy voice say: 'Murderer! Murderer!
You can buy your way out of it this time
but you'll get yours!'

Weeks later Father lay ill in their giant bedroom
drinking crates of Coca-Cola, no way to quench
his thirst: diabetes brought on by shock. Hospital,
tests, new life programme, insulin shots
morning and night, not too much sun, no boozing,
watch that diet. Impossible. The wittiest man
at The Naval and Military Club; soul of the party
at Freshwater Bay Yacht Club; backbone
of 'The Killing Pen' at Steve McHenry's famous pub,
he could not change his habits overnight. So

comas came on. Mother and I forcing sugar in water
down his throat, one on each side of the bed,
passing the glass across hurriedly as he
rolled, getting it into him
for his life's sake.

His brothers flew across Australia to his hospital bed
to force him out of their rich company. He signed.
Pride would not let him fight them off or ask
for help. Doomed by guilt, trapped
by alcohol, sick and tired, he went to bed
yet one more time, this night jellybowls of blood came
jumping out, Mother sick herself on the couch,
I called the doctor. Mother and I rode
in the ambulance, sat in cold hospital corridors
frightened of death. Caught a taxi home,
driver kept Mother downstairs
while I cleaned Father's blood off their bedroom floor
as best I could. My fourteenth birthday. He died
two weeks later. My sick mind cleaned up
as best it could
                    until, wacked on
booze and dope, that night rose again
fifteen years later and drove me
to a cliff's edge where I aimed at the sky.
My car bogged and I ran
to that doctor's house, vomited over him
as he opened his door, 5am, startled.

Woke in hospital. White bed, white walls, blue river
through green pine trees out my window, worried
wife and child at home. I stared, wondering who was I,
asked my tidy shrink for LSD, I wanted it all to rise,
to know the sweetness and horror of all my days.
He controlled me on pills and platitudes.

Photos show a happy man, young wife and son, dressed
Seventies style, fit, smiling, curator
of a writers' cottage by the sea, where
the music of Dylan and Zappa mingled with Miles Davis
beyond the sound of colonial banjos.

Eight months later, dressed in white,
daisychains around our necks and in our hair,
we drove at dawn to
an artist's champagne breakfast in the hills,
giant trees in the yard, minimalist paintings on the walls.
In my mood even eggs-and-bacon looked bohemian
as I drank orange juice, champagne-and-orange,
champagne, then whatever
alcohol I could find . . . Made my usual Jesus jokes
about turning water into wine. Spent late afternoon attempting
to blow up petrol stations across the hills
with lit strips of cloth, laughing uncontrollably at
who knows what . . .

Blackouts returned, fights, lost days of
fear and loathing, my combatant driving . . . I swung
an axe at my love's neck, went to lunch Friday,
came home Sunday, not knowing where I'd been,
who I'd seen, days of life lost. With me late as usual
wife gave up waiting, locked windows and doors.

I slept black nights in a ratty tin shed.

MORE BOOZE

Looking to buy more booze
we cut open the moneybox
that's a Big Red Boomer.
The children count the coins:
their education could be worse.
In the kitchen we total-up
empties. The morning sun
rises to the occasion. Our days
keep their change close. Puns
come soon; then, in
the afternoon, sullen
evening drops in, early.

THE FAMILY ALBUM
for Olive Hale

i)

Tricks of light and mirrors
catch me bare-arsed
on our backsteps

so young I
innocently clutch
my pants in one hand

and wave with the other

ii)

Father in New Guinea
almost tourist shots
with thatched huts

beneath swaying palms
only that one's been
shelled   it's written

in fading pencil on
the back 'just about
gone that time'

iii)

Mother no-one
will believe that's you
so round and smiling

who stands a
matchstick today

iv)

I recoil
from that photo
of whales' blubber

because I remember
coloured slides
Father showed

our lounge room
walls wet with
blood

v)

My twenty first
birthday hair cut
clean shaven

dinner suit bowtie
all for Mother
always for others

vi)

That's my
Rasputin look
my students

dig it out
of a Seventies
anthology and

say 'Dig!'

We're doing
dialects of
decades past

vii)

Hanging on
our walls
they stare

great-grandparents
as babies
wife's grandfather

with long curls
and lace cuffs
who beat your

mother and scared
our children
who spent his

last days
weeping for
. . . himself?

My father sits
by our bed
as a boy

ankles crossed
below fat legs
which later

became his
painful
pins

Your mother on
toes in her tutu —
Miss Albany '31

shows off
her '91
walking frame

Tricks of light
and mirrors now
catch me naked

POEM FOR PIXI

You take me tamely if I let it be,
you say I do, and give me nothing
for my desire. My lust
is a broken winged angel
looking for a home, and I am
wooing who I think you are
as you keep on being so.
You stay, I miss you,
and howl dark plaints
in the cold.

My shed rambles in our backyard
leaning against the wind
and your desire to order
the garden. Could I woo
you better with hammer and nails,
my song all bangings and grunts,
sweat rivulets running
down my arms? Would we roll
about on smooth jarrah boards
wave upon breaking wave of
us?

Would our angels sneer
at our devils sitting
so gloomily inside? They
had us for enough years of
jealousy and rage. Now
this kindly age makes us
mellow, we sit on a sunny porch
and swap tales of childhood.

It is like seeing pictures of us
before we met. Our children now
build their memories to sit
on a future porch speaking
of us, how the shed stayed
in pieces in our backyard
until Dad was inspired to
put it together. Will they then
know the magic spells that let
stories be told, the words for
the songs which all became
beginnings?

I see in your eyes the garden,
shed and our children's play.
My lust remains, reeling
its blue movie, an angel
like a moth dusts the screen
with reassurance. My songs
are sung for wooing you, their rhythm
a randy beat. This love
is a cage should you let me go,
you take me tamely if
I let it be.

THIS PRECARIOUS ACT

She wears a hatrack of faces, all moody.
He swaps a lot himself, on edge,
reacting to her.
To speak of the woe that is Marriage; she?
Naive, his trust in their pledge
was her half-forgotten murmur.

Jobless, broken, out of luck, he
contemplates . . . but no, in his
children he rejoices
each day more. From the sterility
of application and the mys-
tery of rejection he rejuices

in a poem. What's wrong in that? At
times in tears, he keeps sane
through this precarious act,
his face under her hat
on the movable rack. A gain,
some time won, a small tact.

SUNDAY ROAST
for my mother

In this room I surround myself
with books
open like birds in flight

Through my door a smell
of roast
takes me back to childhood

brothers and sisters and I
roamed the house
asking Mother for lunch

as roast potatoes spat
oven door
opened and slammed

gravy's deep brown consistency
stirred
with a flat wooden spoon

Six streets away at Freshwater Bay
Yacht Club
Father stood 'just one more

for the road' Oven was
turned down
afternoon grumbled on

pale-faced plates on the table
knives and forks
straightened again and again

I still have the iron
Father flailed
his carving knife at

in a swashbuckling rhythm which
called us
to lunch 3:45 Sunday

Today I hunger for us
to be
impossibly together again

I close my books and go
walking
this grey day in Spring

DIARY OF A BAD BACK
for my mother

From the library
I borrow 'The End of Senility'
thinking of you
forgetting all the time lately
how you worry about it
so much
it makes forgetting worse . . .

or am I
foolishly
trying to tie the clock's hands
behind its back?

*

At the doctor's surgery
when they ask you
your birth year
you turn to me as if I'd know
'1912? 1913?'
History-book years to me
'Oh, you know . . .'

I know
you let your cat eat
better than you
and report on his health
before your own

I say
you forget *yourself* too much

I wonder
where your piano is now?
Who is learning scales
on your last upright
left in Melbourne
in nineteen forty what?

*

Today your back is worse
you phone to say
you cried this morning

This pre-mourning is
mixed with
pointless anger

a ragbag
of emotions
tossed in despair

*

Again you ring
your back is worse

'Please buy catfood and milk . . .'

I go   I buy   I return
the phone is ringing

You have just rung to say
don't bother
you looked in your fridge
there's enough

You are feeling
so much better now
the cat has eaten

*

X-rays show
your spine is thin
and fractured

Each step
up your stairs
is a new pain

My ragbag is torn

I turn away
and see
my children

waiting
on the first stair

A NIGHT AT THE BEACH

crowded with people
all ages   all manner of dress —
evening gowns   dinner suits
business suits   bikinis
turtle-neck jumpers   torn jeans
biker's leathers   school uniforms

I know them all
they turn their heads
and smile as I pass   my eyes
work like a movie camera
the dream its screen   I sit
in the front row of myself

my grandfathers left
their offices to be here
this hot evening   seagulls fly
like moths about giant beachfront lights
grandfathers take off
three-piece pin-striped ashgrey suits
take off business shirts together
like dancers
old-fashioned singlets and boxer shorts
make tidy mountains of their lives
gold fob watches tock face to face
grandfathers walk to water's edge
naked as the day they were born
now old and grey-haired
with proud upright unironed bodies
skin white as moonlight
side by side lie down and lap
at the ocean like cats

up and down the beach
relatives and friends step out
of photographs and jack-in-the-box memories
take off their clothes
lie to lap salty waters with pink tongues
slowly they form
a fleshly fringe to ocean's shore
small dunes of buttocks white as broken waves
legs all lengths
toes playful in the sand

THE PRESENT PEACE

Let us start
from now —
the present is a gift
to unwrap
like a two-faced game
: clock's hands unwrap
return
we unwrap
pass it back : so
on : until World's end
we merely change
faces : then we shall see
who has won

and won what

AN UNEASY FAITH

BIRTHDAY ANGELS

My childhood favourite
was a heavy black
wooden chair

stumpy carved legs
stood on lion paws
holding their ground

around the flat seat
a hardwood hem
with indented archways

Each birthday
I knocked on
an archway door
seven for my seventh
eight for my eighth

asking a blessing
of my birthday angel

Head propped on hands
I waited   elbows bent
by the lion paws

HALLWAY CHAIR AT MOTHER'S

Everytime I arrive   at Mother's
too long between visits   I run
my hands over   the hallway chair's
round back   to feel the smoothness of
generations of family   to know
the sweat of   hot bodies running in
from summer games _ or cold
bodies wet   from heaven's rain

all of us   come home

BOARDING SCHOOL DAYS

Our Lady of Lourdes stood stony white
between green bushes before
the sandstone school   her outstretched hands
held little pools   her nose twitched
incense mixed with   blood-and-bone

Angelus domini   we prayed
eyes closed   against the sun
priests among us   black crows
We genuflected   a ragged rhythm
hesitant puppets

Early evening threw   powerline pole crosses
across our Golgotha   Christ's disciples with
raspberry jam on our faces   knees bleeding
from asphalt slides in our ball-branding game
all limbs left to heal   blood-and-bone complete

Okay   here we were
early evening   angels again

ANGELS FOR ALICE

Seraphim sing in the flutes
of your bones
Chagall's angels play
your violin

Here are the angels of your moods:
hellfire angel of your
dark anger;
angel of laughter
when your spirit sings;
angel of dance
in your shining grace

You brush their wings
in our kitchen
as you practise
pirouettes

Tribal angels
gossip among us
in this meeting place

ANGELS FOR CHARLIE

Angels are in you
wings open
to embrace the start of day
Angels lift bones
from your bag
of dreams
interconnecting
all working parts
and walk you
to breakfast half awake —
who else pours
the milk? spreads
the jam?

FIRST STONE
Julia's Wedding Anniversary

Willy wagtails flew away for years
now they return   dark and darting

*

She walks down the aisle
uplifted by blossom
from our home tree

Stained glass
throws Christ's shadow
across our shoulders
'May we not stumble
and fall into sin'
The confessional
is a hive

Today
in memory
I skim the first stone
on the still waters
quiet day in August

TOPPLED ANGELS

Mammal fear threw
my angels out
Now each new anxiety
kills another
article of faith

You stayed
through years of
blackouts and speed
angels on
hope

Who sent you here —
my creator, your creator?

Today
my tongues bleed
in the death hour before dawn
I sit in our kitchen and
shiver
in my dressing gown

Love and lust
unglued
veins dry as old vines

Who will take you away —
my destroyer, your creator?

One night   unhinged
I sat on a hospital bed
1am in fright
as death masks of
my living loves
paraded towards me
decomposing as they came

My mind is torn
by its own pain

Who brought me here —
my creator, your destroyer?

THIRD STEP

*'Made a decision to turn our will and our lives
over to the care of God as we understood Him'*

(from The Twelve Steps of Alcoholics Anonymous)

Bread and wine into
body and blood
each priest's daily duty

fingers crocked holding
Christ aloft
like circus jugglers

Sober three months
I searched
for my love of God

In Darlington's cracked
stone church
I recoiled from wine

Switched to Sawyers Valley
Christian Fellowship
where Christ's blood came

in glass thimbles
fresh grape juice
pure and simple
Now ten years sober
this bread and water way

God holds my will

in trust:
He downs my ups
and ups my downs

Everyday I wake
I give
my will away

MIRROR

I swim in a mirror
praying it won't break

Praying in a mirror
God reflects on Himself

Reflecting on God
I swim in a prayer

GREETINGS

OWL ON CADDY'S FARM

On the farmhouse wall
                    hangs
        Caroline's drawing of owl
feathers closed
                wings awkward
        from fall . . .
                    he is
            image of a tree bough
        body
                living woodiness
                    texture
                look of bark
    graphite shadings
                    his eyes
                            see fields
            map the Blackwood River
                                    where it dams
                    and elbows its way
                                    through trees
        He eats mince
    with a piece of loving heart
        cut feather as roughage

                    *

            Three yellow stones
                        dug out of earth
        are stepping stones to the pond where
            a moonlit tantra spot
                    grows in moss

        Owl's mind
                    owns this place

GREETINGS FROM YUNDERUP
for Miles

Night One
moon
chewed small
in the sky.

Moon sits
slight and nervous
at her desk,
evening star
her receptionist.

Where's the white heron?
Out on errands.

*

Sandflat
weeds and grit
ignored by tides
knit together
seeds caught
in wind's hands.

I row through the hair
of Yunderup islands,
strong tides cleansing
the arteries.

*

On small elbows
of the rocky shore

barefoot
tree stands
ankle-deep in its history

tendrils translating

*

Rowing up river
oars slip   pull
unevenly   boat
waggles

Laughing mullet
swim beneath

I sweat and swear
break my back
grimace at the sun

Birds fly over
using air's
currents

I ship oars —
my silent tutors
fly on

*

Swings hang
unswung
on the empty island
Old stove
stares through
pigweed
to sky

Broken slab
cracks into little gardens
New trees
make themselves at home
from old seeds
waiting
beneath the gone floor

Emptying the boat
of rain
we wait for sun

Gumnuts
roll off
the brimless roof

ten years to 2000AD

*

Words
are swept
to shore
in hairtrees
amongst dripping jetties
to whisper
with cobblers
in river reeds

Words fly from
Murray River boatmen

Only crowcalls
from a high nest
in the ragged Norfolk pine
cut through
the norwester

Frogs talk
and their dumb words
climb a jetty
in my skull

*

Day breaks
trees resting
birds asleep in
their nests

Children calm as the river

*

Dandy
stripe-legged spider
set his net last night
now snoozes off breakfast
in his hammock

Blue-backed finch flies
take-away breakfast
to his family
home beneath the jetty

In single column
three pelicans
scoop breakfast
in their big bills

We eat muffins
eggs and bacon with toast
and coffee   instant
in our nest —
twenty dollars a day

*

One dollar buys
20 metres
of fishing line
enough Number 7 hooks
to catch
four trumpeters

Seagulls attend
bloodred beaks
dripping

Pelican swims
grand   aloof   alone

*

I've thought for days
of trade   who does what
for a dollar   how trade
brings people together

Fisherman/shopkeeper nets
the whole affair
with his morning catch

Product/industry/transport/fuel —
commerce is
a pattern of knots

We're caught in our own nets —
habits
and set pieces

PEACEFUL BAY

Two hours down Highway 1
breakfast by roadside

       coffee steam
       mingles
       with morning mist . . .

Donnybrook at dawn

       we take it in turns
       to piss
       in an empty lot
       off Main Street

*

Mist hangs so heavy
road gets lost

headlights cut through
hilly hollows of fog

soup in a bowl

*

We arrive   Peaceful Bay is ripped
by power saws   loud mowers
        cut scrappy lawns   trim edges
owners spend their time
        upkeeping shacks   fishing
            getting pissed

Teenage dudes suck on stubbies
        drive panel vans
                customised   flash

Harold   monochromatic dog
        yaps dawn to dusk
                happy to be here

*

'Come an' have a drink —

got ya stubbyholder?'

*

Lonesome kid kicks a footy
on pebbly 3rd Avenue
(streets named the New York way)

Thong flies with the ball
        like a bird
following its mother close

Peppermint tree takes a high mark
kid yells 'Wot a beauty!'

*

Mushrooms?

We search wet-with-dew-at-noon kikuya grass
lifting an upturned wormholed wooden chest —
        yellow grass beneath
            shrinks back
                surprised —

not one.

Not surprised.

*

'Coffee or tea?
Tea or coffee?'

'Toffee, thanks.'
'Only got honeycomb.'

*

Two peppermints grow out of an old banksia
        translucent pink fingers on red hands

old tree wears a moss shawl
        around hunched stony shoulders

*

Elders of the tribe talk over a ute tray
    stubbies in their hands
sons wear footy guernseys   maroon-&-gold
    black-&-white . . . stubbyholders
carry club emblems   The Lions   The Tigers
    the roar of the crowd
fills their silences . . .

Genesis :: the Family Tree   Pop builds here
    son builds there
                            grandson too young
for footy on 3rd Avenue   watches
    itchy in his thongs   shadowing the play

Smoke flies between shacks   little Meg
    in dusty green Speedo bathers
runs up the pebbly road   slipping
    carrying her dog   pleading
'He's hurt! He's hurt!'

Harold looks amazed   juggled ragtoy

*

Community Noticeboard message:
    'Sharon — Craig not comming today'
speling out wot it sez

*

In the dunes   ants build a dome
of tiny dry sticks . . .
no contract to sign
no shire orders
they build their city
singing with activity

94

ON THE ROAD TO DENMARK

Cows sit on
a dam's ridge
like toys from
a farmyard pack

Big rock mountains
grow out of Earth
like cracked
museum skulls
wrapped tightly to
distend for fashion:

landscape's
old grey brain

*

Denmark Easter Saturday Market:

'Old Tyres Turned Into Beauty'
cut and turned inside-out
and round-about
as swans

painted white with
original tyre-black
showing through
in dramatic effect

We stop and stare.
Children run crazily
caught in Autumn's crossfire
leaves drifting down

*

Straight road
rises   falls
like a slow
sideshow alley
ride:

> NEW WORK
> NO LINES
> MARKED

Everyone writes poems
driving to Denmark
inspired

ALONG THE TIDELINE

fifty snubnosed old tractors line up — Duffields, Massey Harrises, Massey Fergusons, Nelson & Browns — rusty trailers like red tails pointing out to sea . up and down the beach barking kelpies run, crazed by ocean smells and teasing seagulls . women knit seaweed scarves, talking with fish mouths and pink tongues . fat men jostle like jellyfish, dribbling beer from stubbies cooled in rusty Eskys

seagulls stand strong, facing the wind on the rocks above the reef that points into the bay . Mother Dog pisses and a rusty stain runs to the South Pole

aluminium 'Noah's Ark' hoves into view : two metres long, small Evinrude outboard at back . Noah wears old army jumper, floppy khaki hat, faded baggy Hawaiian bathers . today Missus Noah wears a yellow oilskin, her grey hair in a permanent wave

Southern Ocean runs in and out of giggling toes as tiny fish swim in the shallows

fishing fleet appears, all beach people stand up, shade eyes . boats roll in on small surf waves, men jump ashore, self-conscious, busy with ropes, buckets, rods, reels and tackle . they winch boats to tractors, then carry the catch to the cutting bloc — a giant jarrah log that seemingly grows out of the reef—there is no time for beauty here : queen schnapper   swede   black arsed cod   pink salmon   dhu-fish giant red gropers   lose their bright brilliant sea-colours so quickly : knives slice fillets out ... first mate washes white meat in ocean waters off the reef — Yappy Harold slinks off with the skins . audience stands about, stubbies in hand, talking loud to be over-heard : 'just like a cooking demonstration' — 'you don't cut on the rocks unless you cut bloody good' . fish flash fleshy pinks and greens, bright red skins, blue/yellow scrambleline designs, scales 'big as ashtrays' . nullaguy eyes roll cold on the rocks, their surprise swims in the sea

*

tonight
    we eat fruit of the sea
    as heads rolls out
    in the evening
    tide

beside her pillow
    little Meg places
    tiny seashells
    found in giant fish guts

biggest treasure
    on Upper Third Avenue

SUMMER GHAZALS

UNEMPLOYED

I write by processor, wearing my wife's glasses beside
a defrosting fridge :: all these things, yet I am I.

In the Social Security office they are predictable: they
work the system from their side for their security.

All this 'free time'? Is full of fear, doubt, worry. I smile
at the greengrocer, offer him poems for food. No go.

Broke, I send only my 'acceptable' work out, tighten my
critical belt. Editors relax, posties carry a lighter load.

Loving to read, write and discuss, I am defrosting
from an airconditioned man to the poet I am. I am I.

FEAR

Fridge defrosts slowly now night has cooled. Wife, children
asleep, I wonder what dreams unreel in their heads.

Ambulance screams past cemetery to hospital — an image
of ants at wounded ants flashes from childhood. Fear again.

So still, night is dumb. Off the coast a cyclone paces,
choosing a path to cut across the red-dirt north.

Summer is raw. Violence in nightclubs, bars,
bedrooms, kitchens. Lust brings hate to the boil.

Daily the Salvos play carols, door to door. Nightly
the dream is punched out of the children's eyes.

ABSENT FRIENDS

Where do they go when they leave Perth? I read their
work in 'The Australian' but I can't see their eyes.

What values exist there? Does their sundial tell
the same hour? Their crickets click the same song?

Furniture outlives friendship here. You couldn't say 'That's
Viv's chair' because it would be cold before he came back.

And Dorothy will put you in poems but not in the post.
We rely on mail out here in the child-eyed West.

Those who return remark the windy city, hothouse days
that fray the nerves, clusters of writers on brown lawns.

MELROS BEACH
for Jane

Afternoon sun on Melros tints my skin as I walk
among the dead the tide swept up to give us life.

Sea sponges have shapes like clouds, now evoke
the same imagery: bones, breasts and lover's legs.

The forecast is for more of the same. You agree.
Your sky and mine ramble freely, with some cloud.

Can we change? We wish and don't change. Again
we don't know. We try. I look out to sea.

Night crackles. Black sea lights up, all whales,
dolphins and fish electrocuted. We play cards.

TIDES

It is possible I have written too much sadness
to leave it at that who begat what
time has swallowed women swelling through
seasons O my luck to be the broken boy
of mother's blind womb born in open urbanity
so certified in birth my paperlife begins
I have writhen through my first cry in songs
swelling in women and swallowed in whispers
each summer beached in the white belly of years
tears and laughter torn as begat and forgotten
women in season swelling to waves of touch
the sharp skin ache in the weathers of night
chilling the transient dunes in dissolution
a moonlit dome in her shadow play. It is
possible I have not sung enough of love
to reach the swelling of ill reason
my rising tide beached between thighs
begotten in listless waves of two-lip
speakers singing the ocean to shore
between the rolling reefs gone now in
the frightened fish-dash of time shadows
swelling like flesh a woman remembers so
rolls down a dune her swollen ache